Theme Skills Tests
Table of Contents

Colors All Around
Level K, Theme 2
Theme Skills Test Record

Student _____   Date _____

Test Record Form

PART	SCORE	LEVEL OF RESPONSE	RESULT S, D, E, or NE	COMMENTS
A Beginning Sounds (Maximum Score = 5)		4–5 = Strong 2–3 = Developing 1 = Emerging 0 = Not Evident		
B Sequence of Events (Maximum Score = 3)		3 = Strong 2 = Developing 1 = Emerging 0 = Not Evident		
C Making Predictions (Maximum Score = 3)		3 = Strong 2 = Developing 1 = Emerging 0 = Not Evident		
D Initial Consonants: s, m, r (Maximum Score = 5)		4–5 = Strong 2–3 = Developing 1 = Emerging 0 = Not Evident		
E High-Frequency Words: I, see (Maximum Score = 3)		3 = Strong 2 = Developing 1 = Emerging 0 = Not Evident		

Name _____

Beginning Sounds

Practice

 |

1.

 |

Go on

2.

 |

3.

 |

4.

5.

Part A Beginning Sounds _____

B Name_____

Sequence of Events

Practice

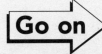

1.

2.

3.

Part B Sequence of Events _____

C Name_____

Making Predictions

1.

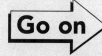

2.

3.

Part C Making Predictions _____

STOP

D Name_____

Initial Consonants: *s, m, r*

Practice

 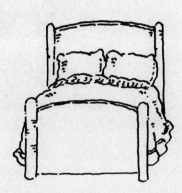 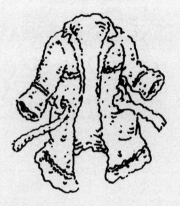

1.

  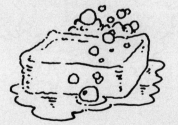

Go on

2.

r | **2**      

3.

m |       

Go on →

4.

r

5.

s

STOP

Part D Initial Consonants: s, m, r _____

Name_____

High-Frequency Words

Practice

I

see

· ·

1.

see

I

2.

I

see

3.

see

I

Part E High-Frequency Words: *I, see* _____

We're a Family
Level K, Theme 3
Theme Skills Test Record

Student _____   Date _____

Test Record Form

PART	SCORE	LEVEL OF RESPONSE	RESULT S, D, E, or NE	COMMENTS
A Beginning Sounds (Maximum Score = 5)		4–5 = Strong 2–3 = Developing 1 = Emerging 0 = Not Evident		
B Story Structure: Characters/Setting (Maximum Score = 3)		3 = Strong 2 = Developing 1 = Emerging 0 = Not Evident		
C Drawing Conclusions (Maximum Score = 3)		3 = Strong 2 = Developing 1 = Emerging 0 = Not Evident		
D Initial Consonants: _t, b, n_ (Maximum Score = 5)		4–5 = Strong 2–3 = Developing 1 = Emerging 0 = Not Evident		
E High-Frequency Words: _my, like_ (Maximum Score = 3)		3 = Strong 2 = Developing 1 = Emerging 0 = Not Evident		

Beginning Sounds

1.

 |

2.

 |

Go on

3.

 |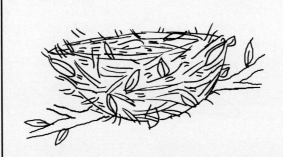

4.

 |

Go on

5.

 |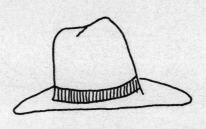

STOP

Part A Beginning Sounds _____

B Name_____

Story Structure: Characters/Setting

1.

Go on ⇒

2.

3.

Part B Story Structure: Characters/Setting _____

C

Name_____

Drawing Conclusions

1.

2.

3.

STOP

Part C Drawing Conclusions _____

Name _____

Initial Consonants: *t*, *b*, *n*

1.

2.

      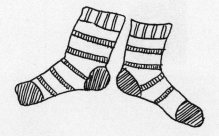

3.

n

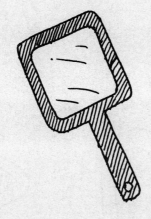 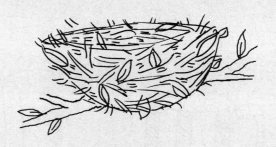 

4.

b

Go on ⇨

5.

 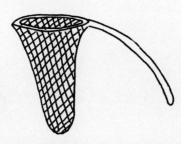  

Part D Initial Consonants: *t*, *b*, *n* _____

High-Frequency Words

1.

my

like

2.

like

my

Go on

3.

my

like

Part E High-Frequency Words: *my, like* _____

Friends Together
Level K, Theme 4
Theme Skills Test Record

Student _____   Date _____

Test Record Form

PART	SCORE	LEVEL OF RESPONSE	RESULT S, D, E, or NE	COMMENTS
A Blending Onset and Rime (Maximum Score = 5)		4–5 = Strong 2–3 = Developing 1 = Emerging 0 = Not Evident		
B Text Organization and Summarizing (Maximum Score = 3)		3 = Strong 2 = Developing 1 = Emerging 0 = Not Evident		
C Cause and Effect (Maximum Score = 3)		3 = Strong 2 = Developing 1 = Emerging 0 = Not Evident		
D Initial Consonants: *h, v, c*; Blending *-at* words (Maximum Score = 5)		4–5 = Strong 2–3 = Developing 1 = Emerging 0 = Not Evident		
E High-Frequency Words: *a, to* (Maximum Score = 3)		3 = Strong 2 = Developing 1 = Emerging 0 = Not Evident		

Blending Onset and Rime

Practice

1.

Go on

2.

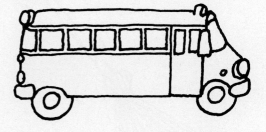  

3.

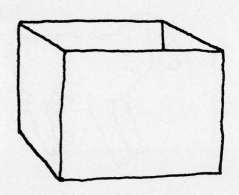  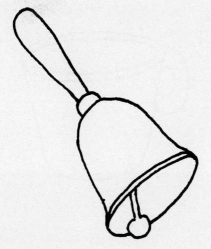

4.

5.

 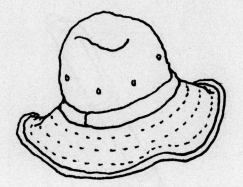 

Part A Blending Onset and Rime _____

B Name_____

Text Organization and Summarizing

1.

 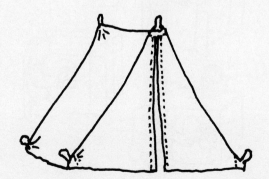 

2.

3.

Part B Text Organization and Summarizing _____

STOP

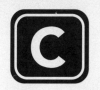

Cause and Effect

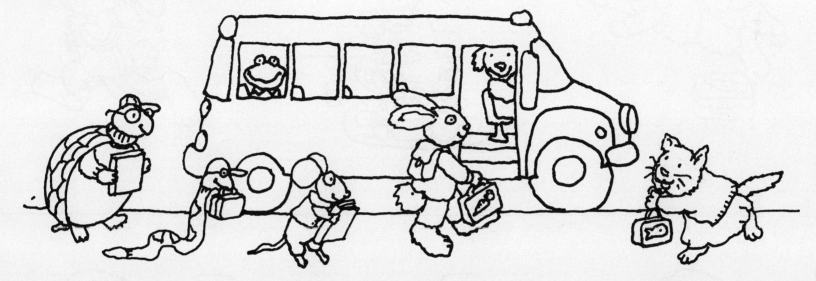

1.

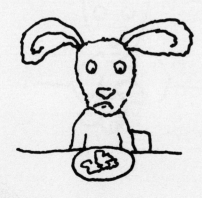 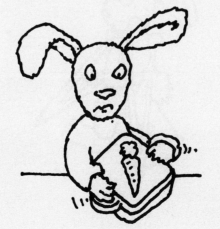 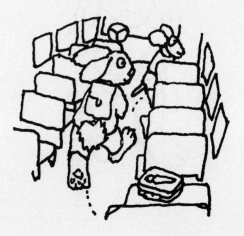

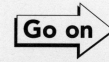
Go on

2.

3.

Part C Cause and Effect _____

Name_____

Initial Consonants: *h*, *v*, *c*; Blending -*at* Words

1.

h

2.

v

 Go on

3.

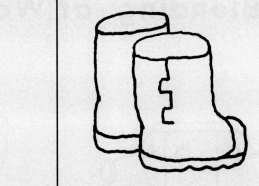  

Part D Initial Consonants: *h, v, c* _____

4. See my hat!

5. I see a cat.

Part D Blending -*at* Words _____

High-Frequency Words

1.

a

to

my

2.

to

like

a

3.

to

a

I

Part E High-Frequency Words: *a, to* _____

Let's Count!
Level K, Theme 5
Theme Skills Test Record

Student _____   Date _____

Test Record Form

PART	SCORE	LEVEL OF RESPONSE	RESULT S, D, E, or NE	COMMENTS
A Blending Onset and Rime (Maximum Score = 5)		4–5 = Strong 2–3 = Developing 1 = Emerging 0 = Not Evident		
B Categorize and Classify (Maximum Score = 3)		3 = Strong 2 = Developing 1 = Emerging 0 = Not Evident		
C Story Structure: Beginning, Middle, End (Maximum Score = 3)		3 = Strong 2 = Developing 1 = Emerging 0 = Not Evident		
D Initial Consonants: _p_, _g_, _f_; Blending _-an_ Words (Maximum Score = 5)		4–5 = Strong 2–3 = Developing 1 = Emerging 0 = Not Evident		
E High-Frequency Words: _and_, _go_ (Maximum Score = 3)		3 = Strong 2 = Developing 1 = Emerging 0 = Not Evident		

A Name_____

Blending Onset and Rime

1.

2.

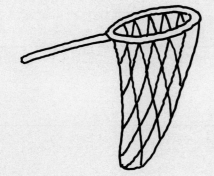 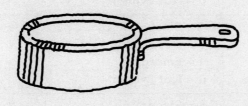 

Go on

3.

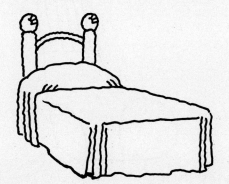

4.

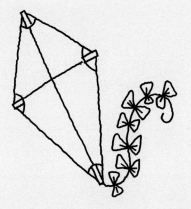

Go on

5.

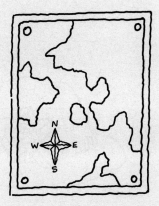 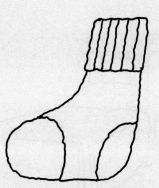 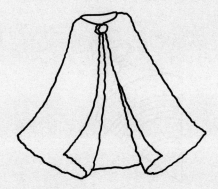

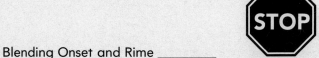

Part A Blending Onset and Rime _____

B Name_____

Categorize and Classify

1.

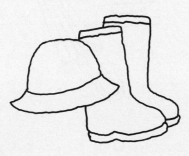

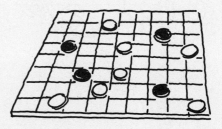

2.

   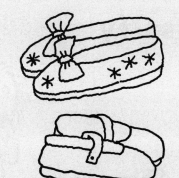   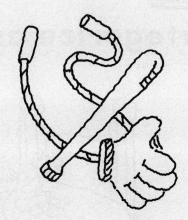

3.

      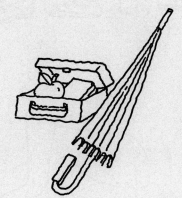

Part B Categorize and Classify _____

Name _____

Story Structure: Beginning, Middle, End

1.

2.

3.

Part C Story Structure: Beginning, Middle, End _____

D Name_____

Initial Consonants: *p, g, f;* Blending *-an* Words

1.

g

2.

p

 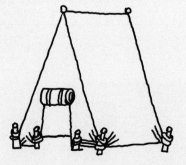 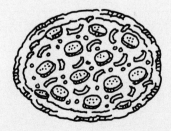

Go on

3.

  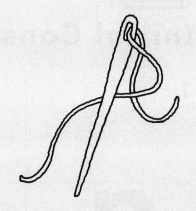

Part D Initial Consonants: *p, g, f* _____

STOP

4. I ran.

5. Nan and I see a man.

Part D Blending -*an* Words _____

High-Frequency Words

1.

go

like

and

2.

and

my

go

Go on ⟶

3.

and

go

a

Part E High-Frequency Words: *and*, *go* _____

Sunshine and Raindrops
Level K, Theme 6
Theme Skills Test Record

Student _____   Date _____

Test Record Form

PART	SCORE	LEVEL OF RESPONSE	RESULT S, D, E, or NE	COMMENTS
A Blending and Segmenting Onset and Rime (Maximum Score = 5)		4–5 = Strong 2–3 = Developing 1 = Emerging 0 = Not Evident		
B Fantasy/Realism (Maximum Score = 3)		3 = Strong 2 = Developing 1 = Emerging 0 = Not Evident		
C Story Structure: Plot (Maximum Score = 3)		3 = Strong 2 = Developing 1 = Emerging 0 = Not Evident		
D Initial Consonants: *l*, *k*, *qu*; Blending *-it* Words (Maximum Score = 5)		4–5 = Strong 2–3 = Developing 1 = Emerging 0 = Not Evident		
E High-Frequency Words: *is*, *here* (Maximum Score = 3)		3 = Strong 2 = Developing 1 = Emerging 0 = Not Evident		

Name_____

Blending and Segmenting Onset and Rime

1.

2.

 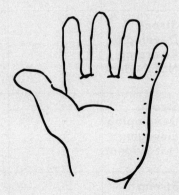 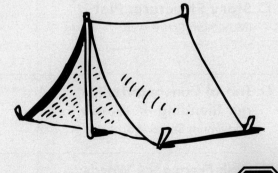

STOP

Practice

··

3.

4.

- -

5.

- -

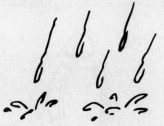  

Part A Blending and Segmenting Onset and Rime _____

B Name_____

Fantasy/Realism

1.

Go on ➡

2.

3.

Part B Fantasy/Realism _____

C Name_____

Story Structure: Plot

1.

2.

3.

Part C Story Structure: Plot _____

Name _____

Initial Consonants: *l*, *k*, *qu*; Blending *-it* Words

1.

k |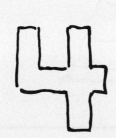

2.

 |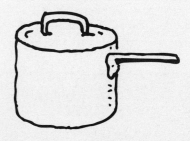

3.

qu

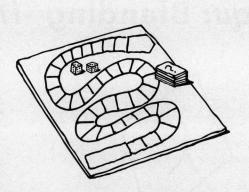  

Part D Initial Consonants: *l*, *k*, *qu* _____

STOP

4. Kit can <u>s</u>it here.

5. I like to <u>h</u>it it.

Part D Blending *-it* Words _____

High-Frequency Words

1.

go

is

here

2.

is

my

here

3.

is

see

here

Part E High-Frequency Words: *is*, *here* _____

Wheels Go Around
Level K, Theme 7
Theme Skills Test Record

Student _____   Date _____

Test Record Form

PART	SCORE	LEVEL OF RESPONSE	RESULT S, D, E, or NE	COMMENTS
A Blending Phonemes (Maximum Score = 5)		4–5 = <u>S</u>trong 2–3 = <u>D</u>eveloping 1 = <u>E</u>merging 0 = <u>N</u>ot Evident		
B Text Organization and Summarizing (Maximum Score = 3)		3 = <u>S</u>trong 2 = <u>D</u>eveloping 1 = <u>E</u>merging 0 = <u>N</u>ot Evident		
C Cause and Effect (Maximum Score = 3)		3 = <u>S</u>trong 2 = <u>D</u>eveloping 1 = <u>E</u>merging 0 = <u>N</u>ot Evident		
D Making Predictions (Maximum Score = 3)				
E Initial Consonants: *d*, *z*; Blending *-ig* Words (Maximum Score = 5)		4–5 = <u>S</u>trong 2–3 = <u>D</u>eveloping 1 = <u>E</u>merging 0 = <u>N</u>ot Evident		
F High-Frequency Words: *for*, *have* (Maximum Score = 3)		3 = <u>S</u>trong 2 = <u>D</u>eveloping 1 = <u>E</u>merging 0 = <u>N</u>ot Evident		

Name_____

Blending Phonemes

Practice

1.

Go on

2.

3.

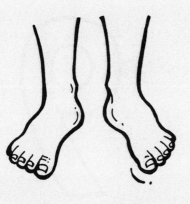  

4.

 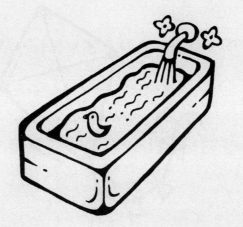 

5.

Part A Blending Phonemes _____

B Name_____

Text Organization and Summarizing

1.

Go on ➡

2.

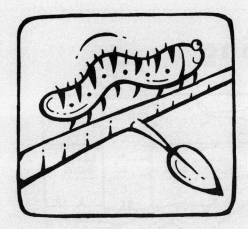  

3.

 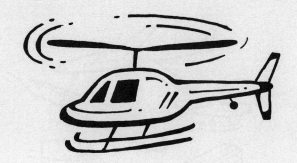 

Part B Text Organization and Summarizing _____

C

Name_____

Cause and Effect

1.

  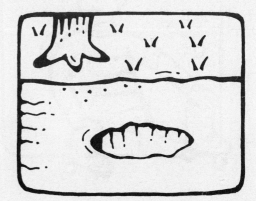

2.

3.

Part C Cause and Effect _____

D Name_____

Making Predictions

1.

Go on

2.

3.

Part D Making Predictions _____

Name_____

Initial Consonants: *d*, *z*; Blending *-ig* Words

1.

d

2.

z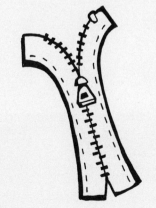

 Go on

3.

d |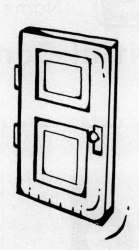

STOP

Part D Initial Consonants: *d, z* _____

4. Here is a big pig!

5. I see a man dig.

Part E Blending -*ig* Words _____

F Name_____

High-Frequency Words

1.

for

here

have

2.

like

have

for

3.

have

to

for

Part F High-Frequency Words: *for, have* _____

Down on the Farm
Level K, Theme 8
Theme Skills Test Record

Student _____   Date _____

Test Record Form

PART	SCORE	LEVEL OF RESPONSE	RESULT S, D, E, or NE	COMMENTS
A Blending Phonemes (Maximum Score = 5)		4–5 = Strong 2–3 = Developing 1 = Emerging 0 = Not Evident		
B Fantasy/Realism (Maximum Score = 3)		3 = Strong 2 = Developing 1 = Emerging 0 = Not Evident		
C Noting Important Details (Maximum Score = 3)		3 = Strong 2 = Developing 1 = Emerging 0 = Not Evident		
D Drawing Conclusions (Maximum Score = 3)				
E Final Consonant: *x*; Blending *-ot* and *-ox* Words (Maximum Score = 5)		4–5 = Strong 2–3 = Developing 1 = Emerging 0 = Not Evident		
F High-Frequency Words: *said, the* (Maximum Score =3)		3 = Strong 2 = Developing 1 = Emerging 0 = Not Evident		

Name_____

Blending Phonemes

1.

   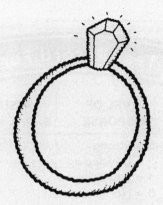   

2.

      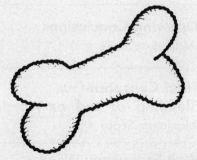

3.

4.

5.

  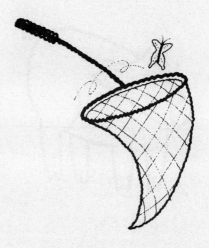

Part A Blending Phonemes _____

Name _____

Fantasy/Realism

1.

Go on

2.

3.

Part B Fantasy/Realism _____

C Name_____

Noting Important Details

1.

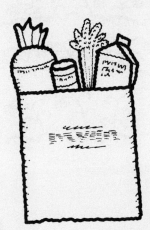      

2.

3.

Part C Noting Important Details _____

Drawing Conclusions

Name_____

1.

Go on

2.

3.

Part D Drawing Conclusions _____

E

Name_____

Final Consonant: *x*; Blending *-ot* and *-ox* Words

1.

X

  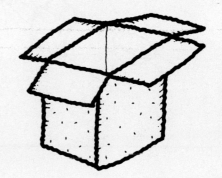

2.

X

Part E Final Consonant: *x* _____

3. Pat said, "It is <u>hot</u> here."

4. I like to see a <u>fox</u>.

Go on →

5. But the fox is <u>not</u> here.

Part E Blending -ot and -ox Words _____

Name_____

High-Frequency Words

1.

said

is

the

2.

the

said

and

3.

have

said

the

Part F High-Frequency Words: *said, the* _____

Spring Is Here
Level K, Theme 9
Theme Skills Test Record

Student _____   Date _____

Test Record Form

PART	SCORE	LEVEL OF RESPONSE	RESULT S, D, E, or NE	COMMENTS
A Blending Phonemes (Maximum Score = 5)		4–5 = <u>S</u>trong 2–3 = <u>D</u>eveloping 1 = <u>E</u>merging 0 = <u>N</u>ot <u>E</u>vident		
B Sequence of Events (Maximum Score = 3)		3 = <u>S</u>trong 2 = <u>D</u>eveloping 1 = <u>E</u>merging 0 = <u>N</u>ot <u>E</u>vident		
C Story Structure: Characters/Setting (Maximum Score = 3)		3 = <u>S</u>trong 2 = <u>D</u>eveloping 1 = <u>E</u>merging 0 = <u>N</u>ot <u>E</u>vident		
D Categorize and Classify (Maximum Score = 3)				
E Initial Consonants: *w, y*; Blending *-et* and *-en* Words (Maximum Score = 5)		4–5 = <u>S</u>trong 2–3 = <u>D</u>eveloping 1 = <u>E</u>merging 0 = <u>N</u>ot <u>E</u>vident		
F High-Frequency Words: *play, she* (Maximum Score = 3)		3 = <u>S</u>trong 2 = <u>D</u>eveloping 1 = <u>E</u>merging 0 = <u>N</u>ot <u>E</u>vident		

Name_____

Blending Phonemes

1.

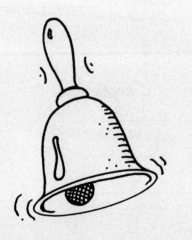 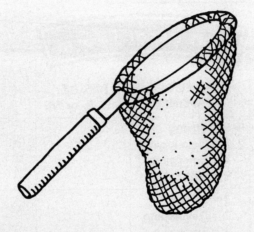 

2.

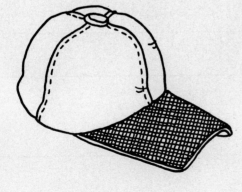  

Go on

3.

 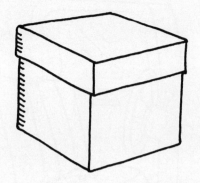 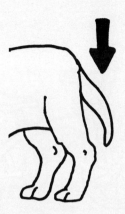

4.

 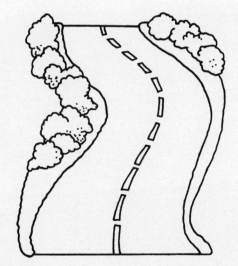 

5.

STOP

Part A Blending Phonemes _____

B Name_____

Sequence of Events

1.

Go on →

2.

3.

Part B Sequence of Events _____

C Name_____

Story Structure: Characters/Setting

1.

2.

3.

Part C Story Structure: Characters/Setting _____

D
Name_____

Categorize and Classify

1.

Go on ➡

2.

3.

Part D Categorize and Classify _____

Name _____

Initial Consonants: *w*, *y*; Blending -*et* and -*en* Words

1.

w

2.

y

Go on →

3.

W

STOP

Part E Initial Consonants: *w, y* _____

4. I have a pet <u>hen</u>.

5. Ben and I get <u>wet</u>.

Part E Blending *-et* and *-en* Words _____

F

Name_____

High-Frequency Words

1.

play

go

she

2.

said

play

she

3.

she

and

play

Part F High-Frequency Words: *play*, *she* _____

A World of Animals
Level K, Theme 10
Theme Skills Test Record

Student _____   Date _____

Test Record Form

PART	SCORE	LEVEL OF RESPONSE	RESULT S, D, E, or NE	COMMENTS
A Blending and Segmenting Phonemes (Maximum Score = 5)		4–5 = <u>S</u>trong 2–3 = <u>D</u>eveloping 1 = <u>E</u>merging 0 = <u>N</u>ot Evident		
B Story Structure: Beginning, Middle, End (Maximum Score = 3)		3 = <u>S</u>trong 2 = <u>D</u>eveloping 1 = <u>E</u>merging 0 = <u>N</u>ot Evident		
C Compare and Contrast (Maximum Score = 3)		3 = <u>S</u>trong 2 = <u>D</u>eveloping 1 = <u>E</u>merging 0 = <u>N</u>ot Evident		
D Story Structure: Plot (Maximum Score = 3)				
E Initial Consonant: *j*; Blending -*ug* and -*ut* Words (Maximum Score = 5)		4–5 = <u>S</u>trong 2–3 = <u>D</u>eveloping 1 = <u>E</u>merging 0 = <u>N</u>ot Evident		
F High-Frequency Words: *are*, *he* (Maximum Score = 3)		3 = <u>S</u>trong 2 = <u>D</u>eveloping 1 = <u>E</u>merging 0 = <u>N</u>ot Evident		

Name_____

Blending and Segmenting Phonemes

1.

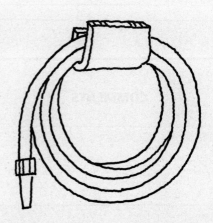 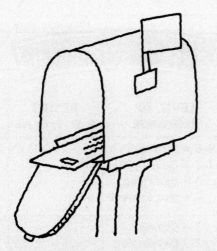 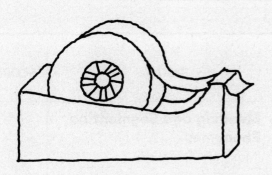

2.

Part A Blending Phonemes _____

STOP

Practice

3.

4.

5.

Part A Segmenting Phonemes _____

STOP

B Name_____

Story Structure: Beginning, Middle, End

1.

2.

3.

Part B Story Structure: Beginning, Middle, End _____

STOP

C Name_____

Compare and Contrast

1.

2.

3.

STOP

Part C Compare and Contrast _____

Theme 10: A World of Animals

Name_____

Story Structure: Plot

1.

Go on →

2.

3.

STOP

Part D Story Structure: Plot _____

Name_____

Initial Consonant: *j*; Blending *-ug* and *-ut* Words

1.

2.

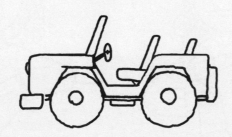  

Part E Initial Consonant: *j* _____

3. See the <u>bug</u> go.

4. She can <u>cut</u> it.

Go on ⟹

5. I like to get a <u>hug</u>.

Part E Blending *-ug* and *-ut* Words _____

F

Name_____

High-Frequency Words

1.

she

are

he

2.

he

go

are

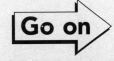

3.

me

he

are

Part F High-Frequency Words: *are, he* _____